Usain Bolt

by Grace Hansen

Abdo
OLYMPIC BIOGRAPHIES
Kids

abdopublishing.com

Published by Abdo Kids, a division of ABDO, PO Box 398166, Minneapolis, Minnesota 55439.

Copyright © 2017 by Abdo Consulting Group, Inc. International copyrights reserved in all countries. No part of this book may be reproduced in any form without written permission from the publisher.

Printed in the United States of America, North Mankato, Minnesota.

102016

012017

 THIS BOOK CONTAINS RECYCLED MATERIALS

Photo Credits: Alamy, AP Images, Getty Images, iStock

Production Contributors: Teddy Borth, Jennie Forsberg, Grace Hansen

Design Contributors: Laura Mitchell, Dorothy Toth

Publisher's Cataloging-in-Publication Data

Names: Hansen, Grace, author.

Title: Usain Bolt / by Grace Hansen.

Description: Minneapolis, MN : Abdo Kids, 2017. | Series: Olympic
    biographies | Includes bibliographical references and index.

Identifiers: LCCN 2016952610 | ISBN 9781680809473 (lib. bdg.) |
    ISBN 9781680809527 (ebook) | 9781680809572 (Read-to-me ebook)

Subjects: LCSH: Bolt, Usain, 1986- --Juvenile literature. | Track and field
    athletes--Jamaica--Biography--Juvenile literature. | Olympic athletes--
    Jamaica--Biography--Juvenile literature. | Olympic Games (31st : 2016 :
    Rio de Janeiro, Brazil)--Juvenile literature.

Classification: DDC 796.42/092 [B]--dc23

LC record available at http://lccn.loc.gov/2016952610

Table of Contents

Early Years

Usain Bolt was born on August 21, 1986. He is from Jamaica. Bolt was racing by age 12.

Florida

Jamaica

5

Bolt did not qualify for the 2004 Olympics. Injuries held him back. He could not run in full **pro** seasons for a few years. But he continued to work hard.

By 2007, Bolt had recovered.

He beat the Jamaican

200-meter record.

Beijing!

In 2008, Bolt competed at the Olympics in Beijing. He ran in the 100- and 200-meter events. He broke the world and Olympic records in both!

10

11

World Champ!

Bolt went to the 2009 World Championships. He ran the 100- and 200-m sprints. He beat his world records! He ran his best 100-m in 9.58 seconds.

12

13

London!

In 2012, Bolt broke his Olympic record. He ran the 100-m in 9.63 seconds. He won gold in his other events, too.

Rio!

Rio 2016 was Bolt's third Olympics. He was going for the **triple-triple**!

16

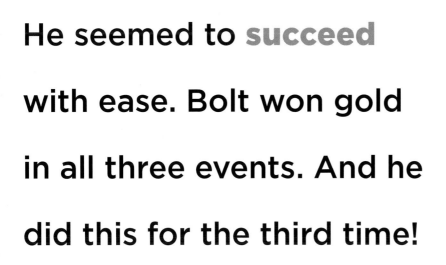

He seemed to **succeed** with ease. Bolt won gold in all three events. And he did this for the third time!

19

The Lightning Bolt

Bolt shocks the world with his amazing speed. That's why he is called the Lightning Bolt!

More Facts

- Bolt won his first Olympic gold medal with his shoelaces untied.

- Bolt claims that he has never run a full **consecutive** mile in his entire life.

- Bolt is 6 feet 5 inches (196 cm) tall, making him taller than most sprinters. This means he can run 100m with fewer **strides**. On average, Bolt takes 41 strides. Other sprinters take around 45.

Glossary

consecutive – following each other continuously.

pro – short for professional.

stride – a long step.

succeed – to achieve the desired result.

triple-triple – winning the 100-, 200-, and 4x100-meter relay races in three consecutive Olympics.

Index

abdokids.com

Use this code to log on to abdokids.com and access crafts, games, videos, and more!

Abdo Kids Code:
OUK9473